Measuring Up

Assessment Tools for Volunteer Programs

by Steve McCurley & Sue Vineyard

Published by:

Heritage Arts Publishing
1807 Prairie Avenue
Downers Grove, IL 60515

The *Volunteer Marketplace*, a free catalogue of publications from Heritage Arts, is available by calling (800) 272-8306 or by faxing a request to (703) 803-9291.

Other books by Sue Vineyard and Steve McCurley which are available through the *Volunteer Markeplace* include:

- *Stop Managing Volunteers! New Competencies for Volunteer Administrators*
- *Volunteer Management: Mobilizing All the resources of the Community*
- *Megatrends and Volunteerism: Mapping the Future of Volunteer Programs*
- *Evaluating Volunteers, Programs, and Events*
- *Managing Volunteer Diversity: A Rainbow of Opportunities*
- *101 Ideas for Volunteer Programs*
- *101 More Ideas for Volunteer Programs*
- *101 Tips for Volunteer Recruitment*
- *101 Ways to Raise Resources*
- *Marketing Magic for Volunteer Programs: How to Get What and Who you Need*
- *Beyond Banquets, Plaques & Pins: Creative Ways to Recognize Volunteers*
- *Secrets of Leadership*
- *Secrets of Motivation: How to Get and Keep Volunteers and Staff*
- *How to Take Care of You, So You Can Take Care of Others*
- *The Great Trainers Guide: How to Train (almost) Anyone to Do (almost) Anything*

In addition, *Grapevine*, a bi-monthly newsletter on volunteer involvement edited by Sue and Steve is available for subscription from the *Volunteer Marketplace*

Table of Contents

How to Tailor the Materials in This Book

The forms used in this booklet are here for you to use as given or to tailor to your own needs.

Frequently we have added some background statement at the top of a form to simply lay the groundwork of information you need as you use the instrument.

For example in the form labeled "Assessing Motivations: Matching People and Work," the opening paragraphs give you a very brief explanation of the Motivational Theory of David McClelland.

In using this assessment you would probably omit this background information and either photocopy the lower portion of the form or rewrite it to perhaps add jobs and language peculiar to your own setting for respondents to assess.

For material such as the "Workshop Evaluation Form," you may wish to use it as is but add a second page that gets to information you need to have about a specific workshop. An example might be a fifth section on technical or procedural information imparted.

Please consider each of the forms that follow "drafts" for you to use as best fit your own needs. We consider each of you a potential co-author with us and welcome your creativity!

Steve McCurley and Sue Vineyard

Assessment of Agency Readiness for Volunteers

❑ Does the organization have a clearly defined mission with long-range goals which relate to the community?

❑ Have staff and volunteers been involved in developing the plan to accomplish these goals and have they considered and discussed the involvement of volunteers in accomplishing the mission of the agency?

❑ Is the volunteer work to be done meaningful? Is it useful and significant to the agency, program, and clients?

❑ Can the need for the job be adequately explained to a potential volunteer? Can we describe how this job contributes to the mission of the agency?

❑ Can the work be done by a volunteer? Can it be reasonably be split into tasks that can be done on evenings or weekends? Is it amenable to a part-time situation? Are the needed skills likely to be available from volunteers, or can people be easily trained in the knowledge and background needed?

❑ Is it cost effective to have the work done by volunteers? Will we spend more time, energy and money to recruit, orient, and train volunteers that we would if we utilized staff? Are we looking at volunteer involvement on a long-term or short-term basis?

❑ Is a support framework for the volunteer program in existence? Do we have a person ready to act as volunteer manager, volunteer policies and procedures, and inclusion of the volunteer program in the agency plan and budget?

❑ Are staff willing to have the job done by volunteers? Do all staff understand their roles in relation to the utilization of volunteers? Can we explain to volunteers what their roles will be in working with staff?

❑ Can we identify volunteers with skills to do the job? Are they likely to be available in our community?

❑ Will people want to do this volunteer job? Is it a rewarding and interesting job or have we simply tried to get rid of work that no one would really wants to do, paid or unpaid?

❑ Do we know what we will do with the volunteers after we get them? Do we have adequate space for them? Do we know who is in charge of them? Does that person know what they are doing?

❑ Do we know how we will evaluate success and how and to whom feedback will be given?

❑ Is, in the end, the agency committed to the involvement of volunteers or is someone just looking for a "quick fix" solution to their problem?

Staff Assessment Survey on Volunteer Involvement

As part of our agency plan to utilize volunteer assistance, we would like you to complete the following questionnaire. This survey is designed to assess our readiness to use volunteers and to determine what we need to do to ensure continued delivery of high quality services to our clientele. All of the information collected will be kept confidential.

I. Experience with Volunteers

1. Have you previously worked in an agency which involved volunteers?

    ❑ Yes   ❑ No   ❑ Don't Know

2. Have you previously supervised any volunteers?

    ❑ Yes   ❑ No   ❑ Don't Know

3. Do you do any volunteer work yourself?

    ❑ Yes   ❑ No   ❑ Don't Know

    If "Yes," please briefly describe your current volunteer activities:

II. Assessment of Volunteer Involvement

1. What is your overall assessment of the desirability of utilizing volunteers at this time?

    ❑ Very desirable   ❑ Somewhat desirable   ❑ Uncertain

    ❑ Not desirable at this time   ❑ Would never be appropriate

2. What is your overall assessment of our current readiness to utilize volunteers?

    ❑ Very ready   ❑ Somewhat ready   ❑ Uncertain   ❑ Not Ready

3. Are there any areas or types of work for which you think that volunteers are particularly needed and suited in our agency?

4. Are there any areas of the organization or types of work which you think that volunteers should not be involved with in our agency?

5. What issues or concerns would you like to see addressed before we involve volunteers?

6. What type of training or assistance would you like to receive before staff are asked to work with volunteers?

7. Are there any other comments, concerns, or questions that you would like to express about the involvement of volunteers in our agency?

Checklist Prior to Recruitment

❑   Have we consulted with staff who will be working with this volunteer?

❑   Are the staff clear on what their role will be in working with the volunteer?

❑   Is there a complete and accurate job description written for the position?

❑   Does the position description clearly identify the qualifications for the job and outline both the purpose and nature of the work to be done?

❑   Have we identified a work environment for the volunteer, including a supervisor, work space, etc.?

❑   Do we have a good idea of what kind of volunteer would be suitable for this position?

❑   Do we have a good idea of what kind of applicant would not be suitable?

❑   Have we determined the kinds of questions and screening procedures we would use to examine applicants?

❑   Do these questions really determine whether the volunteer will have the ability and interest to perform the work?

❑   Do we know how we will compare candidates?

❑   Do we know who will participate in the interviews?

❑   Do we know what we will do with "rejected" candidates?

❑   Do we know what volunteer benefits will be offered with this position?

❑   Do we have a plan for orienting and training this volunteer?

❑   Have we analyzed risk factors of the position and developed a risk management plan?

❑   Does our plan of recruitment relate to this kind of volunteers? Are both the appeal we will be using and the distribution plan for information appropriate?

Checklist for a Volunteer Recruitment Message

✓ The opening of the Message is interesting enough to entice the potential volunteer to continue reading or listening. The body of the Message is appealing enough to interest the potential volunteer in considering the volunteer opportunity or, at least, in contacting the agency to get more information. Boring Messages are only likely to appeal to boring people.

✓ The body of the Message presents information in an order that psychologically matches how people will think about the offer:

❑	Need:	*Is there a problem?*
❑	Solution:	*Can this job help solve it?*
❑	Fears/Questions:	*Will I be capable of helping with it?*
❑	Benefits:	*What's in it for me?*
❑	Contact Point:	*How do I get involved?*

As a general rule, spend more space on need than on logistics. People will first decide whether you're worth volunteering for and then decide whether they can fit you into their schedule. The need you stress may be yours, your clientele's, or a perceived need/benefit of the volunteer.

✓ The Message is easily understood. The Message is intelligible and avoids jargon, unless it is included for a specific reason. The Message has been tested for ease of comprehension by someone other than the author of the Message. Remember: *What Can be Misunderstood, Will Be.*

✓ The Message has been tested on members of the target group at whom it is aimed, to make sure it is understandable to them and communicates in a way most likely to be appealing to their interests.

✓ The Message gives a complete picture: clientele, type of work, requirements, timeframe, person to talk with. The Message doesn't make the potential volunteer have to do any extra work in order to understand what is going on.

✓ The contact information for the Message gives the name of a person, preferably including their first name, not just the name of the agency. Volunteering is a personal decision and people like to talk with other people about it.

Assessing Motivations: Matching People and Work

Just as people have different motivations, so do tasks. According to David McClelland, people most concerned with relationships ("Affiliators") love jobs where they can interact with others and hate those that keep them alone in a back room copying figures; those most concerned with tasks ("Achievers") will often take the same back room job over having to be greeting people at the front door of the church; those most concerned with influencing others ("Empowerers") would forego either of the mentioned jobs in favor of being on a Board and persuading the town to hold a walkathon! Knowing a person's predominant motivation (we are all three, but one predominates) helps in matching them to a job that fits. As any volunteer leader will tell you, recruiting someone is not the real trick, keeping them is. The best way to do this? Match people to compatible jobs!

Check the things below that interest you most. There are no "wrong" answers; every response is "right." They are categorized under the three labels shown above. Be honest; give your first reaction.

Affiliation motivated people enjoy:

Task forces	Committee work	Supervisors as friends	Working with Clients
Talking on the phone	Recruiting others	Group projects	Writing personal notes
Social opportunities	Family gatherings	Advising personally	Case-work
Mentoring	Welcoming new people	Celebrations	Outreach programs
Visiting	Listening	Parties	Meeting folks
Recognition events	Orientation	Colleagues	Job-sharing
Collaboration	Relationships	Having a fat Rolodex	Partnering

Achievement motivated people enjoy:

Gathering statistics	Leading events	Details	Fundraising
Seeing trends	Keeping records	Supervisors as guides	Setting records
Auditing	Being a treasurer	The shadows	Filing
Leading meetings	Being alone	Keeping score	Quiet time
Making connections	Technology	Advising professionally	Information
Documentation	Skill-building tasks	Parameters	Goals & objectives
Job descriptions	Assessments	Checkpoints	

Power motivated people enjoy:

Challenges	Impossible dreams	Solving disputes	New ideas
What's never been done	Innovation	Lecturing	Creating
The spotlight	Authority positions	Board positions	Publicity
Leveraging	Teaching	Titles	Influencing others
Convincing	Fundraising	Writing articles	Supervisors who go away
Strategizing	Friendraising	Consulting	Leadership
Inside information	Recruiting	Other power people	

You will probably note that you have more checks in one category than the other two, but checks in all three. If you have about an equal balance of checks in all three, it simply means that you will probably be satisfied with a wide variety of jobs.

Placement Checklist for Community Service Students

This checklist must be completed and turned into the supervising teacher **before** the student reports to the community service assignment.

		Yes	No
1.	Do you know exactly what is expected of you in performing the assignment?	❑	❑
	Do you have these expectations in writing?	❑	❑
2.	Do you know who is responsible for supervising your activities?	❑	❑
3.	Do you know:		
	• What you can do if you have a problem with your assignment?	❑	❑
	• Who has the right to change your activities?	❑	❑
	• Where you will be working?	❑	❑
	• How you will get to and from your work site?	❑	❑
4.	Do you know how your performance is to be evaluated?	❑	❑
5.	Have you informed your school or agency of any special problems or medical condition that should limit you or be taken into account in your participation?	❑	❑

This form is due by: _____

_____   _____
Signature of Student   Date

_____   _____
Signature of Parent   Date

_____   _____
Signature of Teacher   Date

Student's Name: _____
                                          (Please Print)

Checklist for a Volunteer Orientation Session

✓ Description of agency purpose and mission.

✓ Brief history of the agency.

✓ Description of programs and services to clientele.

✓ Explanation of special needs of clientele.

✓ Explanation of commonly used jargon and acronyms.

✓ Sketch of organizational chart and introduction of key staff.

✓ Timelines and description of major organizational events and activities.

✓ Orientation to the facilities and equipment.

✓ Introduction to organizational etiquette:

- forms of address of staff and clients
- appropriate behavior standards
- appropriate dress
- confidentiality of client information
- time constraints: absences, tardiness, etc.

✓ Description of volunteer program procedures:

- recordkeeping requirements
- training schedule
- supervisory relationships
- risk management practices
- evaluation process
- benefits

✓ Explanation of what a volunteer should do if they run into any problems.

Volunteer Training Design Worksheet

1. Who are the individuals/positions/groups to receive training? What are their previous levels of involvement with this subject or with the requirements of this job?

2. What *information, experience,* and *attitudes* do we wish each to have at the ending of the training?

A. *Information* may include knowledge of the project and the system, knowledge about the position or the recipients of the service, "how-to's" related to the position's functions or specific skills:

    1.

    2.

    3.

B. *Experience* may include practice at being someone (such as through role-playing or role discussion) or practice at doing something (such as constructing a tentative plan of action or operating equipment).

    1.

    2.

    3.

C. *Attitudes* may include a clear sense of purpose and direction, a sense of their ability to do the work well, or the motivation to do the job correctly and according to established procedures.

    1.

    2.

    3.

3. In what order does the above material need to be presented in order to be useful and understandable?

4. What are the available formats for delivery of training?

    ✓   Self-study

        ❑ Videotape
        ❑ Book/manual
        ❑ Magazine/newsletter
        ❑ Web page

    ✓   One-to-one assistance

        ❑ Telephone technical assistance
        ❑ Mentor/buddy system
        ❑ Assigned staff/volunteer coach
        ❑ Apprenticeship

    ✓   Training event/workshop

        ❑ Lecture
        ❑ Exercise
        ❑ Role play
        ❑ Group discussion
        ❑ Case study
        ❑ Worksheet development

5. What format best matches each of the informational, experiential, and attitudinal needs that have been identified?

    a.   Format:

    b.   Format:

    c.   Format:

6. Who should be involved in designing and delivering each component of the training? Consider the desirability of "insiders" versus "neutrals," needed facilitative skills, technical knowledge and experience, and ability to build credibility or to forge relationships.

7. Who else needs to be involved or informed to make this training work in the real world?

❑   Supervisors

❑   Co-workers

❑   Clients

❑   Other:

Training Event Facilities Checklist

- ❏ Adequate space for group.
- ❏ Correct table set-up.
- ❏ Right number of chairs.
- ❏ AV equipment: operational status, correct placement, intelligent operator.
- ❏ Extension cords
- ❏ Electrical outlets
- ❏ Placement of lighting and light switches
- ❏ Screens for AV equipment
- ❏ Temperature controls and ventilation
- ❏ Restrooms
- ❏ Table for registration
- ❏ Table for display materials
- ❏ Podium
- ❏ Name tags
- ❏ Roster and addresses of attendees
- ❏ Flip chart and easel
- ❏ Markers
- ❏ Tape
- ❏ Coat racks
- ❏ Policy on smoking, with suitable facilities
- ❏ Parking information
- ❏ Directional signs
- ❏ Handouts
- ❏ Schedule for breaks
- ❏ Watch or clock

Workshop Evaluation Form

Seminar/Workshop Title: Date:

Trainer(s):   Audience:

Topics:

Rank the following from 1(no value) through 8 (highest value):

I. Workshop as a whole:

	No Value						Highest Value	
1. Topics were clearly addressed	1	2	3	4	5	6	7	8
2. Trainer(s) knew subject	1	2	3	4	5	6	7	8
3. Goal was clear to me in advance	1	2	3	4	5	6	7	8
4. Presentation was clear & organized	1	2	3	4	5	6	7	8
5. Presentation style was good	1	2	3	4	5	6	7	8

Comments:

II. Learning methods:

	No Value						Highest Value	
1. There was a good mix of methods	1	2	3	4	5	6	7	8
2. Visuals were clear & appropriate	1	2	3	4	5	6	7	8
3. Handouts were useful & used well	1	2	3	4	5	6	7	8
4. Lecture was informative & helpful	1	2	3	4	5	6	7	8
5. Good summaries were offered	1	2	3	4	5	6	7	8
6. Media/electronic use was helpful	1	2	3	4	5	6	7	8

Comments:

Measuring Up:

III. Physical setting:

	No Value						Highest Value	
1. The training site	1	2	3	4	5	6	7	8
2. Training room	1	2	3	4	5	6	7	8
3. Breaks well placed	1	2	3	4	5	6	7	8
4. Snacks provided	1	2	3	4	5	6	7	8
5. Length of training	1	2	3	4	5	6	7	8
6. Staff support to assist trainees	1	2	3	4	5	6	7	8

Comments:

IV: Pre-training preparation:

	No Value						Highest Value	
1. I was informed of the topic & goal accurately	1	2	3	4	5	6	7	8
2. I should have been a participant	1	2	3	4	5	6	7	8
3. I received the information I needed to participate	1	2	3	4	5	6	7	8
4. I was given a clear picture of site & surroundings	1	2	3	4	5	6	7	8

Comments:

Three or more key learnings I gained from training:

1.

2.

3.

Suggestions for further trainings:

Checklist Prior to Delegation

Planning the Assignment
I have carefully considered:

- ❑ the purpose/goal of the work
- ❑ a completion date
- ❑ required standards of performance
- ❑ parameters for the work
- ❑ degree of delegated authority
- ❑ budgetary authorization
- ❑ degree of communication/involvement with me or with others
- ❑ the fact that the assignment may be done differently than if done by me personally

Selecting the Person to Do the Assignment
I have carefully considered:

- ❑ who is most interested in doing the work
- ❑ who has the most ability to get the job done
- ❑ who has the personal contacts to get the work done amicably
- ❑ who will find the work challenging and an opportunity for advancement
- ❑ who can fit the work into their schedule with least disruption

Making the Assignment
In making the assignment, I have:

- ❑ carefully described the purpose/goal of the assignment
- ❑ explained the parameters of the work: budget, timeframe, other considerations
- ❑ explained the degree of independent authority that is being granted
- ❑ agreed on communication checkpoints
- ❑ outlined available resources: finances, additional help
- ❑ explained relationships with others who will be involved

Checking the Assignment
In following up, I have:

- ❑ informed others of the delegated authority
- ❑ set reasonable timelines and reporting schedules
- ❑ listened carefully to the opinions of the person to who the work is delegated
- ❑ allowed room for creative thinking in accomplishing the assignment
- ❑ provided follow-up support and encouragement
- ❑ remained open to the need to make changes in the delegated assignment
- ❑ intervened only if there is some absolute necessity and then with minimal interference

Host Agency Responsibilities Checklist

Specific responsibilities will differ among host agencies; however, there are several general responsibilities that apply to all participating host agencies. Each host agency has the responsibility to:

❏ Be prepared and staffed to work with volunteers on a timely basis.

❏ Provide the volunteers with necessary training and information so that they can perform at the expected level.

❏ Provide supervision and guidance.

❏ Provide volunteers with a safe work environment and reliable and functional equipment.

❏ Evaluate performance at regular intervals and share feedback with the volunteers.

❏ Provide liability insurance that covers the volunteers while working with the agency.

❏ Give the volunteers a significant, challenging, and enriching experience.

❏ Give the volunteers the opportunity to work directly with people and to provide needed social services.

❏ Give the volunteers significant responsibilities that will enable them to use their talents and skills.

❏ Be prepared to deal with health or injury problems and with other emergencies.

❏ Work with the volunteers and program coordinators in the event of problems or difficulties.

❏ Write a recommendation for the volunteers if requested.

Volunteers participating in the community service activities should be provided with opportunities that enable them to:

❏ Provide productive and meaningful service.

❏ Increase awareness of social issues in the community.

❏ Gain experience with career options.

❏ Increase awareness of and appreciation of community needs.

❏ Gain experience with evaluation and feedback.

❏ Improve problem-solving and decision-making skills.

❏ Have opportunities for developing new skills.

Staff Assessment of Volunteer Involvement

This form is to allow you to provide feedback regarding our utilization of volunteers. Please answer all questions as completely as possible. Do not sign the survey unless you wish to. All responses will be kept confidential.

1. Are volunteers involved in your area of direct responsibility or in your department?

   ❑ Yes ❑ No ❑ Don't know

2. In your experience, are the volunteers with our agency adequately qualified to perform their work?

   ❑ Yes ❑ No ❑ Don't know

3. Are the volunteers with our agency adequately trained for their responsibilities?

   ❑ Yes ❑ No ❑ Don't know

4. How would you describe the utilization of volunteers in our agency by other staff?

   ❑ Well utilized ❑ Generally well utilized, but some poor use

   ❑ Generally not well utilized ❑ Don't know

5. Do you think our staff has received adequate training in how to work with volunteers?

   ❑ Yes ❑ No ❑ Don't know

6. What else should be done to help our staff work better with volunteers?

7. How would you describe the reaction of our clients to the volunteers?

   ❑ Favorable ❑ Mixed ❑ Unfavorable ❑ Don't know

8. What benefits do you think we have gained from the utilization of volunteers?

9. What problems have we created with the use of volunteers?

10. How has your own work load changed as a result of our utilizing volunteers:?

    ❑ Lessened   ❑ Remained the same
    ❑ Increased   ❑ Changed in type of work done

11. How would you describe the assistance you have received from the volunteer management department?

    ❑ Helpful   ❑ Not helpful ❑ Haven't made use of help

12. Use the space below to make any comments regarding our involvement of volunteers, any additions you would like to make to your answers above, or any suggestions you have about how we might make better use of volunteers.

Volunteer Assessment of the Volunteer Program

As part of our continued effort to improve our volunteer program, we would like your responses to the following questions. All responses will be kept completely confidential. Do not sign the survey unless you wish to.

1. How long have you been volunteering with us?

2. To what extent do you think that volunteers are well accepted by the staff at our agency?

   ❏ Well accepted   ❏ Generally well accepted, but some exceptions
   ❏ Not well accepted   ❏ Generally not well accepted, but some exceptions

3. To what extent do you think volunteers are involved in decisions that will affect their volunteer work?

   ❏ Well involved   ❏ Sometimes involved   ❏ Not well involved

4. To what extent do you think volunteers are accepted and welcomed by clients?

   ❏ Well accepted   ❏ Mixed reception   ❏ Not well accepted

5. To what extent do you think volunteers feel comfortable with the assignments they are given?

   ❏ Comfortable   ❏ Not very comfortable   ❏ Don't know

6. Do you feel that volunteers receive sufficient orientation about our agency before they begin work?

   ❏ Yes   ❏ No   ❏ Don't know

7. Do you feel that volunteers receive enough training to carry out their assignments?

   ❏ Yes   ❏ No   ❏ Don't know

8. In your experience, does your volunteer job match the job description you were given?

   ❏ Yes   ❏ Used to match job description; doesn't now
   ❏ No   ❏ Not given job description

9. Do you find your volunteer work to be interesting, challenging, and rewarding?

    ❑   Yes   ❑   Somewhat   ❑   No

10. Do you think that volunteers are provided with sufficient feedback by those they work with?

    ❑   Yes   ❑   No   ❑   Somewhat   ❑   Don't know

11. Do you think volunteers have sufficient opportunity to advance in responsibility in this agency?

    ❑   Yes   ❑   No   ❑   Don't know

12. Can you think of any new areas or new jobs in which volunteers might be of help to our agency?

13. Can you suggest any ways that we might use to recruit new volunteers?

14. What's the best experience you've had while volunteering for us?

15. What's the worst experience?

16. If you could make three changes in our volunteer program, what would they be?

   1.

   2.

   3.

17. Overall, how would you rate our volunteer program? (Please circle. 1 = Terrible; 7 = Great)

         1   2   3   4   5   6   7

18. Use the space below to make any other comments regarding our utilization of volunteers, or any additions you would like to make to any of your answers above.

Thanks for your help!

Volunteer Position Feedback and Evaluation Form

Name of Volunteer: _____ Period covered:

Position: _____ Date of evaluation:

Supervisor: _____

I. Position Goals:

	Not Met		Satisfactory		Superior
1.	1	2	3	4	5
2.	1	2	3	4	5
3.	1	2	3	4	5
4.	1	2	3	4	5
5.	1	2	3	4	5

2. Work Relationships:

	Needs Improvement		Satisfactory		Excellent
a. Relations with other volunteers	1	2	3	4	5
b. Relations with staff	1	2	3	4	5
c. Relations with clients	1	2	3	4	5
d. Meeting commitments on hours and task deadlines	1	2	3	4	5
e. Initiative	1	2	3	4	5
f. Flexibility	1	2	3	4	5

3. Comments by supervisor regarding above areas:

4. Comments by volunteer regarding above areas:

5. Most significant achievement during period of evaluation:

6. Major area in which improvement, change, or further training would be desirable, with description of suggested course of action:

7. Overall, how does the volunteer feel about remaining in this position? What change in nature of responsibilities or procedures would improve the ability of the volunteer to contribute to the agency?

8. What are the major goals for the volunteer to accomplish in their position between now and the next evaluation period?

     1.

     2.

     3.

     4.

     5.

9. Other recommendations or comments:

10. Scheduled date of next evaluation:

Student Volunteer Self-Evaluation Form

How Am I Doing?

- ❑ Do I offer my services when there is an obvious need for help?

- ❑ Do I accept criticism and suggestions without becoming emotionally upset?

- ❑ Do I follow directions?

- ❑ Do I ask for additional instructions when I do not understand what to do?

- ❑ Do I have a friendly attitude with the agency staff, volunteers, other students and clients?

- ❑ Am I reliable? Do I meet work commitment on time?

- ❑ Am I punctual? Do I show up at my worksite at the designated day and time each week?

- ❑ If I am unable to serve at a designated time, do I give my volunteer manager at the agency a call explaining my absence in advance?

- ❑ Do I listen to those whom I am helping?

- ❑ Do I listen to those who are trying to help me?

- ❑ Do I avoid criticism of the agency, volunteer manager, fellow volunteers, staff or clientele?

- ❑ Do I observe my clientele to know their dislikes, likes, preferences, enthusiasms, aversions, etc.?

- ❑ Do I follow through on all work assignments?

- ❑ Do I try to take a positive approach to problems even when frustrated?

- ❑ Do I take personal responsibility for doing the best job that I possibly can?

Community Service Program Evaluation

Name: _____

Agency: _____

Agency Volunteer Program Manager: _____

1. How many hours do you work weekly?

2. Briefly describe what you do as a volunteer:

3. Did you receive adequate orientation/training before your assignment?

        Yes ❑   No ❑

Comments:

4. What aspects of your volunteer service have not been enjoyable?

5. What aspects of your volunteer service have been most beneficial to the people served?

6. In what way has your experience as a student volunteer been meaningful?

7. Overall, was your time well spent as a student?

8. Will you continue as a volunteer in your community?

        Yes ❑   No ❑

Assessment of Community Service Experience

Instructions: The following describes some possible features of a volunteer experience. Please describe your particular experience by circling the appropriate number from 1 to 5.

		Sometimes Often	Fairly Often	Very	Practically Never	Once in a While
1.	I have enough work to keep me busy.	1	2	3	4	5
2.	The work I do is interesting.	1	2	3	4	5
3.	The work is challenging.	1	2	3	4	5
4.	I've been trained enough to do the work I'm assigned.	1	2	3	4	5
5.	I do things myself instead of just observing.	1	2	3	4	5
6.	I have significant responsibilities.	1	2	3	4	5
7.	I am learning things that will help me in the future.	1	2	3	4	5
8.	I am given clear directions.	1	2	3	4	5
9.	I have a variety of tasks to do at the site.	1	2	3	4	5
10.	Staff take a personal interest in me.	1	2	3	4	5
11.	I have freedom to develop and use my own ideas.	1	2	3	4	5
12.	I am helping people or improving my community.	1	2	3	4	5
13.	My job is just busy work.	1	2	3	4	5
14.	The site is a safe place to work.	1	2	3	4	5
15.	I feel appreciated.	1	2	3	4	5
16.	I get help when I need it.	1	2	3	4	5
17.	I discuss my experiences with my supervisor or co-workers.	1	2	3	4	5
18.	I feel I'm doing a good job.	1	2	3	4	5

My overall rating of my placement(s) at this point is: (Check one)

❑ Excellent   ❑ Good   ❑ Fair   ❑ Poor   ❑ Terrible

Assessment Tools

Exit Interview Questionnaire

We are always striving to improve the performance of our volunteer involvement system. As one of our volunteers, we would appreciate your help in identifying areas in which we might do better. Please be as complete and honest as you can in answering the following questions - all of the information collected will be kept strictly confidential, but it will be utilized to ensure that others who volunteer will receive the best possible treatment.

1. Approximately how long did you volunteer with us?

2. In general, what type of volunteer work did you do with us?

3. Why are you leaving? (Please check all that apply.)

    ❑ Job accomplished   ❑ Moving to new location   ❑ Need a change

    ❑ Didn't like job I was given   ❑ Didn't feel welcome   ❑ Didn't feel well utilized

    ❑ Other time commitments   ❑ Other:

4. What did you like best about volunteering with us?

5. What suggestions would you make for changes or improvements in our volunteer effort?

6. Overall, how would you rate your experience in volunteering with us?

    Terrible   *Average*   *Great*

     1   2   3   4   5

Thanks for your help in completing this form and during your volunteering with us. We appreciate the help you've given us in trying to better assist our clients and our community.

Assessing Volunteer Recognition Efforts

Date: *Organization:*

1. Formal Recognition now used with volunteers and staff: (banquets, pins, plaques, certificates, etc.)

2. Informal Recognition now used: (Name tags, birthday cards, notes of praise, friendly hello, etc.)

3. Ways we get feedback from volunteers/staff on recognition efforts:

4. Recognition efforts once done that might be appropriate again:

5. Recognition efforts we have done for years that may need to rest for a while:

6. Ways to solicit creative new recognition ideas from workers:

7. Ways to insure that a variety of recognition options are used so that differently-motivated people will find some efforts appealing. (Motivations: Affiliation, Achievement, Power.)

8. What ideas can be added to the mix of recognition that can be fun? Meaningful? Long-lasting?

9. Other Suggestions:

Identification of Risks Worksheet

Use this worksheet to brainstorm possible areas of risk related to a volunteer position. Consider possible risks or problems that might arise in each of the categories below:

Physical Ability:

1.

2.

3.

4.

5.

Skills/Knowledge:

1.

2.

3.

4.

5.

Attitude, Maturity:

1.

2.

3.

4.

5.

Equipment Use:

1.

2.

3.

4.

5.

Worksite:

1.

2.

3.

4.

5.

Clientele:

1.

2.

3.

4.

5.

Failure to Follow Procedures:

1.

2.

3.

4.

Risk Assessment Planning Worksheet

Volunteer Job:

Identified Major Risks of this Position:

1.

2.

3.

4.

5.

6.

Special Measures to be Undertaken in Screening Volunteers for Position:

1.

2.

3.

4.

5.

Special Measures to be Undertaken in Training Volunteers for Position:

1.

2.

3.

4.

5.

Special Measures to be Undertaken in Supervision of Volunteers in Position:

1.

2.

3.

4.

5.

Assessment of Need for Volunteer Insurance

- ❏ Is there a clear risk present to the volunteer or others?
- ❏ Is the risk significant in terms of potential damage?
- ❏ Is there some significant likelihood of risk occurring?
- ❏ Is some significant amount of harm or damage likely to occur if an incident happens?
- ❏ Can we better handle the risk by alleviating the condition that causes it?
- ❏ Can we better handle the risk by improved selection of qualified volunteers?
- ❏ Can we better handle the risk by increased training of volunteers and staff?
- ❏ Can we change work procedures to better handle the risk?
- ❏ Can we develop systems to minimize the impact of harm caused by risk?
- ❏ Is the volunteer already protected by personal insurance coverage?
- ❏ Can we obtain coverage more cheaply by reimbursing the volunteer for personal insurance coverage?
- ❏ Can we add the volunteer to existing coverage of the agency or staff?
- ❏ Could we join with other agencies in purchasing this insurance?

Assessment of Volunteer Management Practices

Indicate which of the following volunteer management practices are followed on a regular basis in your agency:

	Yes	No	Don't Know	Doesn't Apply
1. Overall Written Agency Policy on Volunteers	❏	❏	❏	❏
2. Inclusion of Volunteer Involvement as Part of Organizational Plan	❏	❏	❏	❏
3. Involvement of Volunteers in Developing Organizational Plan	❏	❏	❏	❏
4. Long-Range Plan for Volunteer Program	❏	❏	❏	❏
5. Specific Individual Designated to Oversee Volunteer Involvement	❏	❏	❏	❏
6. Sufficient Clerical Support and Equipment	❏	❏	❏	❏
7. Separate Budget for Volunteer Program Coordination	❏	❏	❏	❏
8. Budgeted Funds at Individual Department Level for Volunteers	❏	❏	❏	❏
9. Regular Reports on the Volunteer Program to the Board	❏	❏	❏	❏
10. Written Volunteer Policies and Procedures	❏	❏	❏	❏
11. Formal Staff Training in Volunteer Management	❏	❏	❏	❏
12. Mention of Volunteers in Union Contract	❏	❏	❏	❏
13. Written Job Descriptions for Volunteers	❏	❏	❏	❏
14. Annual Update of Job Descriptions for Existing Volunteers	❏	❏	❏	❏
15. Wide Range of Types of Volunteer Jobs	❏	❏	❏	❏
16. Involvement of Volunteers on Evening and Weekends	❏	❏	❏	❏
17. Minimum Time Commitment for Volunteers	❏	❏	❏	❏
18. Written Volunteer Recruitment Plan	❏	❏	❏	❏
19. Use of Mass Media Recruitment Techniques (TV, Radio Ads)	❏	❏	❏	❏
20. Organized Outreach Efforts to Diversify Volunteer Recruitment	❏	❏	❏	❏
21. Organized Peer Recruitment Effort	❏	❏	❏	❏
22. Formal Interview Process for Potential Volunteers	❏	❏	❏	❏
23. Participation of Staff in Volunteer Interviews	❏	❏	❏	❏
24. Criminal Record Checks of Potential Volunteers	❏	❏	❏	❏
25. Reference Checks of Potential Volunteers	❏	❏	❏	❏
26. Health Screening of Potential Volunteers	❏	❏	❏	❏
27. Probationary or Trial Period for New Volunteers	❏	❏	❏	❏

28. Written Agency/Volunteer Agreement   ❏   ❏   ❏   ❏

29. Formal Volunteer Orientation & Training Session   ❏   ❏   ❏   ❏

30. Involvement of Staff in Orientation & Training Sessions   ❏   ❏   ❏   ❏

31. Designated Supervisor for Each Volunteer   ❏   ❏   ❏   ❏

32. Participation of Volunteers in Staff Meetings   ❏   ❏   ❏   ❏

33. Scheduled Performance Review Sessions with All Volunteers   ❏   ❏   ❏   ❏

34. Confidential Personnel Record on Each Volunteer   ❏   ❏   ❏   ❏

35. Volunteer Involvement in Evaluating Staff   ❏   ❏   ❏   ❏

36. Written Staff Assessment of Volunteer Program   ❏   ❏   ❏   ❏

37. Written Volunteer Assessment of Volunteer Program   ❏   ❏   ❏   ❏

38. Annual Volunteer Recognition Event   ❏   ❏   ❏   ❏

39. System for Informal Day-to-Day Recognition of Volunteers   ❏   ❏   ❏   ❏

40. Recognition of Staff Who Involve Volunteers   ❏   ❏   ❏   ❏

41. Volunteer Recordkeeping System   ❏   ❏   ❏   ❏

42. Statistical Analysis of Volunteer Contribution to Agency   ❏   ❏   ❏   ❏

43. Reimbursement of Volunteer Expenses   ❏   ❏   ❏   ❏

44. System for Recording Cash Contributions of Volunteers   ❏   ❏   ❏   ❏

45. Written Risk Management Plan for the Volunteer Program   ❏   ❏   ❏   ❏

46. Insurance Coverage for Volunteers   ❏   ❏   ❏   ❏

47. Formal Volunteer Exit Interview   ❏   ❏   ❏   ❏

48. Preferential Hiring of Staff with Volunteer Experience   ❏   ❏   ❏   ❏

49. Use of Volunteers to Assist the Volunteer Manager   ❏   ❏   ❏   ❏

50. Use of Volunteer Management Computer Software   ❏   ❏   ❏   ❏

Volunteer Program Statistical Analysis Profile

A.   Average number of volunteers in program during past year: [Check one.]

❑   Fewer than 10
❑   10 to 49
❑   50 to 99
❑   100+

B.   Approximate percentages of volunteer jobs for your agency in each of the following categories:

%

1.   One-time [once a year]   _____

2.   Occasional [three or four times a year]   _____

3.   Short-Term [less than six months]   _____

4.   Long-Term [one year or longer]   _____

5.   Other   _____

                                                              100%

C.   Approximate percentage of volunteers utilized in each category. For first seven categories, indicate only those volunteers who spend the *majority* of their time performing that function; otherwise list in category 8. Please read all categories before starting to determine percentages.

%

1.   Work One-to-One with Individual Client   _____

2.   Work Directly with Many Clients   _____

3.   Work in Group Projects (construction, special events)   _____

4.   Assist Staff (work as staff aide, little client contact) _____

5.   General Community-Wide Service (public information, speakers bureau)   _____

6.   Fundraising (other than as a member of the board)   _____

7.   Board or Committee Work (involved with policy making)   _____

8.   All Around Volunteer (does a little of everything)   _____

                                                              100%

D. How many different types of volunteer jobs are performed in the agency? [Another way to answer this is to determine how many different volunteer job descriptions you have or how many different titles for volunteer positions.]

E. What were the three most interesting or innovative jobs performed by volunteers for your agency during the past year?

1.

2.

3.

F. Of the volunteers utilized last year, what percentage had been volunteering with the agency:

		%
1.	Less than 6 Months	_____
2.	6 Months to less than 1 Year	_____
3.	1 Year to less than 5 Years	_____
4.	5 Years to less than 10 Years	_____
5.	10 Years +	_____

G. Volunteer Tenure: Of the volunteers utilized last year, what percentage had been volunteering with the agency:

		%
1.	One Shot Job (one day or weekend)	_____
2.	Less than 6 Months	_____
3.	6 Months to less than 1 Year	_____
4.	1 Year to less than 5 Years	_____
5.	5 Years to less than 10 Years	_____
6.	10 Years +	_____
		100%

H.   Volunteer Turnover: What percentage of volunteers left the agency in the past year, and thus had to be replaced or re-recruited?

I.   What percentage of the volunteers are in the following demographic categories?

    1.   Age: %
        a.   Less than 14 years   _____
        b.   14 to 17 years   _____
        c.   18 to 25 years   _____
        d.   26 to 44 years   _____
        e.   44 to 64 years   _____
        f.   65+ years   _____

    2.   Gender: %
        a.   Male   _____
        b.   Female   _____

    3.   Race: %
        a.   White   _____
        b.   African-American   _____
        c.   Asian-American   _____
        d.   Native-American   _____
        e.   Hispanic   _____

J.   What percentage of staff people in the agency work with or supervise volunteers?

K.   In which aspects of volunteer management are staff typically involved? By 'typically involved' we mean that this would be normally expected of any staff person who was involved in working with volunteers.

☐   Developing new positions for volunteers
☐   Developing criteria for volunteers considered for these positions
☐   Assisting in volunteer recruitment
☐   Interviewing volunteers
☐   Providing an orientation to new volunteers
☐   Developing components of volunteer training
☐   Providing training to volunteers
☐   Directly supervising volunteers
☐   Participating in volunteer evaluations
☐   Participating in volunteer recognition

Assessment Tools   **35**

L. Volunteer utilization patterns by department/project:

		Utilizes Volunteers	*# of Volunteers*
a.	Board	❑	_____
b.	General Administration	❑	_____
c.	Fundraising	❑	_____
d.	Volunteer Coordination	❑	_____
e.	_____	❑	_____
f.	_____	❑	_____
g.	_____	❑	_____
h.	_____	❑	_____
i.	_____	❑	_____

M. Does your program record the total volunteer hours contributed during the year?

❑ No   ❑ Yes

If yes, what was the total for each of the past three years?

1.

2.

3.

N. Does your program calculate an hourly value for volunteer time?

❑ No   ❑ Yes   If yes, how is this value calculated?

O. Does your program calculate the expense of maintaining the volunteer program?

❑ No   ❑ Yes

If yes, what was the total for each of the past three years?

1.

2.

3.

P. Is the calculated value for the volunteer program regularly included in the financial audit of the agency?

❑ No   ❑ Yes

Assessing Organizational Norms

The unwritten rules that govern behavior in any climate are called "norms". It is critical to understand which norms are at work in your workplace. Norms are found in the four dimensions of climate: *Energy, Distribution of Energy, Pleasure* and *Growth*. Keep in mind that these rule are perceived as real by workers.

I. Energy Norms: How would you characterize the norms surrounding the Energy level in your program? (circle those that best describe your climate. You will probably have a mix of high/low.)

Low energy climate:	*High energy climate:*
"Cool it"	"Go! Go! Go!"
Loose, relaxing style of management.	High competition between workers.
People don't feel involved in work.	People feel very involved.
Very routine; everything is rote.	High tension; conflict.
Change is not allowed.	Change is constant.
People do as little as possible.	People keep doing more than asked.
People feel unimportant.	People feel important.
Other:	Other:

II. Distribution of Energy Norms: Where people must spend their energies determines to great measure how healthy the climate is in a program. You can assess personally which of the following are positive for your setting and which are negative. Check those that best characterize your workplace. People spend their energy and time:

- ❑ *Just trying to survive.*
- ❑ *Being creative.*
- ❑ *Innovating.*
- ❑ *Doing the best job possible.*
- ❑ *Doing short-term work.*
- ❑ *Taking risks.*
- ❑ *Beating the system.*
- ❑ *Doing long-term development.*
- ❑ *On start-up activities.*
- ❑ *On paper work.*
- ❑ *On rote work.*
- ❑ *In inappropriate competition.*
- ❑ *Having to "play games."*
- ❑ *Avoiding conflict.*
- ❑ *Juggling demands.*
- ❑ *In meetings.*
- ❑ *With clients & direct work.*
- ❑ *Working together.*
- ❑ *Socializing.*
- ❑ *Making a difference.*

Some of the above will be positive, negative, neutral and variable among different people.

III. Norms that relate to Pleasure: How it "feels" in an organization relates directly to how pleasurable it is for people to be there. On a scale of 1-9, rate, based on your perspective, how you believe the following aspects of your workplace offer pleasure. Have everyone assess the climate from their perspective; compare perspectives. Discuss ways to reshape work for greater pleasure and comfort. Identify those aspects you cannot change, mapping out options to tolerate them better or reshape them enough to make them acceptable.

	Displeasure							*High Pleasure*	
1. Structure:	1	2	3	4	5	6	7	8	9
2. Policies:	1	2	3	4	5	6	7	8	9
3. Co-workers:	1	2	3	4	5	6	7	8	9
4. Informal rules:	1	2	3	4	5	6	7	8	9
5. Systems:	1	2	3	4	5	6	7	8	9
6. Freedom to be creative:	1	2	3	4	5	6	7	8	9
7. Physical setting:	1	2	3	4	5	6	7	8	9
8. Reward & Recognition:	1	2	3	4	5	6	7	8	9
9. Training:	1	2	3	4	5	6	7	8	9
10. Vision or Purpose:	1	2	3	4	5	6	7	8	9
11. Actual work:	1	2	3	4	5	6	7	8	9
12. Work evaluation:	1	2	3	4	5	6	7	8	9
13. Leadership:	1	2	3	4	5	6	7	8	9

How is *humor* received in your organization? Is it appropriate?

What is *fun?*

IV. Norms related to Growth: When people feel satisfied because they have been able to grow in their work, there is high worker satisfaction which contributes to a healthy climate. What opportunities do people have in your organization to: (rate 1-9)

	None								*Many*
1. Develop new skills:	1	2	3	4	5	6	7	8	9
2. Share new ideas:	1	2	3	4	5	6	7	8	9
3. Suggest change:	1	2	3	4	5	6	7	8	9
4. Innovate:	1	2	3	4	5	6	7	8	9
5. Experiment:	1	2	3	4	5	6	7	8	9
6. Acquire training:	1	2	3	4	5	6	7	8	9
7. Brainstorm:	1	2	3	4	5	6	7	8	9
8. Share deeply:	1	2	3	4	5	6	7	8	9
9. Express individuality:	1	2	3	4	5	6	7	8	9
10. Hold different opinions:	1	2	3	4	5	6	7	8	9
11. Choose work options:	1	2	3	4	5	6	7	8	9
12. Design flex-time:	1	2	3	4	5	6	7	8	9
13. Work in teams:	1	2	3	4	5	6	7	8	9

What actions are rewarded? (formally or informally)

What actions are punished? (formally or informally)

What key words would you use to describe your climate? Why?

What style of management is predominate in your organization? Is this positive or negative?

How to assess responses:

Only you can assess the positive or negative aspects of your workplace. Rules of thumb might be:

#1:   If you have more positive responses for Energy & Energy Distribution, your perception is that your climate is a good one where people can feel useful, productive and engaged in meaningful work.

#2:   If you have high scores for Growth & Pleasure, you think it basically feels good to work there.

Assessing the Health of Your Climate

The productivity and success of an organization is in direct relationship to the health of the "climate" or "feel" of the workplace. This tool helps you assess your organizational climate. In follow-up to using this with yourself and others, identify those factors which are productive and those which are negative, fortifying the former and discarding the latter.

Rate all of the following statements regarding your work place as follows:

1 = Never   2 = Sometimes   3 = Often   4 = Almost Always

	Rating	Category
1. I love going to my work		PC
2. Offices/workstations are personalized by workers		C
3. It's easy for workers to find private space		C
4. My own work space can be as private as I need it to be		PC
5. Workers seem happy working there		C
6. There is pleasant but appropriate chatter		CB
7. You hear people laughing		C
8. When someone comes up with a new idea, people welcome & consider it fairly		B
9. Trust levels are high		B
10. It's OK to "play" with ideas and concepts		AB
11. People are evaluated fairly...the focus is on efforts not personalities		B
12. I feel challenged by my work.		PABC
13. New people are welcomed and assimilate easily		C
14. New workers are brought in with sensitivity to how they will fit in w/ others		BC
15. There is a feeling of teamwork and/or "family"		B
16. Energy is spent on working toward the mission		B
17. The organization's mission is clear and part of all major considerations		B
18. Workers interact with clients or services		C
19. Paperwork is kept at a minimum		PB
20. Rules are enforced fairly and kindly		BC
21. Communication is open and honest between all levels of people		BC
22. Gossip is not necessary. Information is available openly		B

23. Workers socialize after hours _____ C

24. I can express my needs and feelings honestly with my supervisor _____ PB

25. Workers celebrate the success of others _____ CD

26. When problems arise we look to those involved for answers _____ B

27. Blaming individuals is avoided. Energy is directed toward solutions _____ B

28. People around me are my friends _____ PC

29. My work makes good use of my time and talents _____ PB

30. Personal lives are respected _____ CB

31. Questioning of anything is OK _____ BA

32. Blind compliance is NOT valued _____ B

33. There are frequent opportunities to learn new skills _____ D

34. Training is highly valued _____ D

35. Workers and hierarchy mix easily. Leaders seem like "real people" _____ B

36. We have readily accessible tools to tell us what to do when problems arise _____ B

37. "But we always" is NOT considered a valuable response. _____ AB

38. When things go wrong, we stop and fix them. We constantly improve because of this _____ AB

39. Things feel "upbeat" around our site _____ A

40. Change is regarded as positive _____ BC

41. People are involved in decisions that effect them _____ PCB

42. Leaders are fair and ethical _____ B

43. We have fun working together _____ V

44. What I do makes a real difference _____ PAB

45. Preferential treatment is avoided _____ A

46. Hiring practices are fair. _____ A

47. It's challenging for me to work in my organization _____ PB

48. Rewards are appropriate and often personalized to the recipient _____ C

49. Recognition is given freely and creatively _____ CB

50. Workers are corrected quickly to redirect their actions _____ B

51. Rules make sense _____ BC

52. I feel recognized and valued by leadership _____ PABC

53. It's possible to grow in my surroundings _____ PD

54. Quality is valued in all we do _____ A

55. We frequently try new things _____ B

56. I feel my job is secure _____ PABC

57. Minorities are included fairly in our organization _____ BC

58. Diversity is seen as good _____ AB

59. Systems support our work & are changed if they begin to inhibit goals _____ B

60. Job assignments and timelines are clearly defined _____ B

61. Conflict is NOT always considered "bad". Resolution is sought fairly _____ ABC

Total Score:

SCORING
If your total score is:

- 179 - 244   Sounds like a great place to work. Stay!
- 105 - 178   With some effort it can be a great place to work.
- 80 - 104   Oops....problems need immediate attention. If not addressed you'll be in deep trouble.
- 61 - 79   Yikes...your climate is **already** in deep trouble; decide if it can be fixed and how.

CODING CATEGORY
Questions are coded A, B, C, D or P. These codes translate to:

A   Energy level;
B   Distribution of Energy;
C   Pleasure;
D   Growth
P   *your personal feelings about working in your setting*. Consider these carefully.

Add the "**P**" scores (13 of them) up. If your score is:

36 -52   Count your blessings and stay put unless you get an offer of a zillion dollars a year! (Even then, think twice!)
24 - 35   Not bad and could get better...hang in there!
17 - 23   You are not happy; fix it if you can or consider moving on.
16 or less   You may be putting yourself in danger of severe burnout & stress. Get some counseling, consider your options and do what is best for you.

Assessing Your Public Image

It is critical to know what the public thinks of you. Too often, agencies or organizations believe that everyone knows about them, understands what they do and how to become involved. It is simply not true in many cases. Use this form to measure public perception.

Agency/Program Name:

1. Have you heard of this organization before?

2. What do you know/think it does?

3. Who does it serve?

4. Does it use volunteers in doing its work?

5. Where is it located?

6. How long has it been in business?

7. Who runs it? Do you know the name of one of its leaders? Who?

8. How is it funded?

9. Is it a private, governmental or non-profit organization?

10. Does it have a good reputation?

11. Has any scandal ever been attached to it that you can personally recall?

12. Does it produce any products? What?

13. What services does it perform?

14. Is it important to the overall well-being of our community?

15. If a group or individual wanted to become involved as a supporter or volunteer, how would they?

16. Is this an ethical group?

17. Does it use its money well?

18. Does it sponsor any events in the community? Which ones?

19. Do you trust this organization?

20. Would you like more information on this organization?

21. What is your general opinion of this group and what it does?

Assessing The Potential for Successful Change

We are surrounded by change. Certain factors within a workplace setting can forecast how successfully change can be introduced and achieved. Before initiating change, refer to this assessment and modify your efforts accordingly.

Factor	Not True	Somewhat True	Mostly True	Very True
When change is proposed people affected are fully informed				
People know how success will be measured				
We have a history of successful change				
The trust level in our organization is high				
Workers and managers work as a team productively				
Volunteers and staff trust each other and work as a team.				
We have learned from changes that were not successful				
Open dialogue about possible disruptions is encouraged				
When people run into trouble during changes they can ask for help.				
People managing the change care about how it impacts people implementing it.				
The reasons for change are carefully explained				
During explanations leaders make sure through feedback that their message has been understood				
When problem arise during change, leaders are open to suggestions to alter implementation.				
When problem arise, people avoid blaming.				
Successful change efforts are acknowledged and				
celebrated.				
When conflicts arise, they are handled quickly and fairly. Real issues are uncovered and dealt with.				
The reasons for change are given; goals are clear				
The benefits of change are clearly communicated				
People understand what their position will be during and after change				
People know who they will be working with during and after change.				
People who work hard on the change are rewarded				

Assessment Tools

- Changes are thoroughly planned and and thought out
- People who feel negative about change are listened to and have their concerns addressed
- People who work against change are reprimanded
- Training is offered to help people cope with change
- Training is offered to people who will take on new responsibilities because of change.
- People who will have new supervisors after change are given a chance to get to know the new person
- How people feel about change is heard and acknowledged
- People typically feel excited and positive about the future.

Total Checkmarks:

Score:

Score 0 for each *Not True*
Score 2 for each *Somewhat True*
Score 3 for each *Mostly True*
Score 5 for each *Very True*

Analysis:

0-50   You many wish to delay the change until greater trust factors are implemented. Success is not probable if you try to force this change.

50-70   There are some issues that could undercut successful change; address and fix them.

70 & up   You will probably be successful! Good factors will support the change.

Assessment of Need for a Meeting

When to Have a Meeting

✓ You want information or advice from the group
✓ You want to involve the group in solving a problem or making a decision
✓ You need to get a sense of the mood of the group
✓ You want to build a sense of group identity and solidarity
✓ There is an issue that needs to be clarified
✓ You have concerns you want to share with the group as a whole
✓ You wish to share information in a manner which provides more emphasis than in a written communication
✓ The group itself wants a meeting
✓ There are conflicts or differences of opinion amongst group members that need to be brought to the surface
✓ Timing of decisions requires a meeting at this point
✓ There is a problem that involves people from different groups
✓ You need group support for a decision or action
✓ There is a problem and it's not clear what it is or who is responsible for dealing with it

When Not to Have a Meeting

✗ There is no real reason for having the meeting
✗ There is no agreed-upon leader for the meeting
✗ There is no agreed-upon agenda for the meeting
✗ There is inadequate information or poor communication about the topic to be discussed
✗ There is inadequate time for you or for group members to prepare for the meeting
✗ Key participants will be unable to attend the meeting
✗ Something could be communicated better by telephone, memo, or a one-to-one discussion
✗ The subject matter is so confidential or secret that it can't be shared with some group members
✗ Your mind is made up and you have already made your decision
✗ The subjects to be discussed do not interest, involve or affect all of the group
✗ The subject is trivial
✗ There is too much anger and hostility in the group and people need time to calm down before they begin to work collaboratively

Checklist for Effective Meetings

Before the Meeting

✓ Make sure that you have a real reason for meeting
✓ Send out minutes of last meeting as soon as possible after the meeting
✓ Send out a pre-meeting agenda item request form soliciting input
✓ Send out confirmation of meeting site and timeframe
✓ Check with all officers and committee chairs for input on agenda
✓ Encourage committee chairs to provide a brief written report in lieu of a long boring oral report at the meeting; keep oral presentations to items which require a decision or to questions about the written report
✓ Determine agenda and assignments for the meeting
✓ Send out agenda and supporting reports and information
✓ Arrange meeting logistics: room, materials, refreshments, equipment
✓ Determine if there are any problems that will probably arise during the meeting, and devise a plan for how these will be addressed

On the Meeting Day

✓ Arrive early and double-check all logistical arrangements
✓ Bring duplicate copies of materials for participants who did not receive them or who left them at home; bring extra copies for visitors
✓ Start on time even if some members are not present
✓ Stay on time, if at all possible. If the timeframe looks impossible to maintain, get group to consciously consider changing agenda to maintain timeframe
✓ Follow the agenda, both in content and time allocation, unless new information or an emergency warrants alteration
✓ Ensure that important decisions are recorded accurately
✓ Determine clearly who will be held responsible for what delegated actions
✓ Set timeframe for reporting back on actions that are delegated
✓ Strive to make decisions rather than deferring or avoiding controversial items: if it is important, it won't go away; if it is not important, you shouldn't waste any more time with it
✓ Strive for participation from all attendees
✓ Set time, date, and location of next meeting

After the Meeting

✓ Collect written reports given during the meeting
✓ Prepare minutes of meeting for distribution
✓ Start all over again

Assessing Meetings

Meetings have become a way of life in many organizations, and a major source of complaint for those having to stop work assignments to attend. Before having a meeting, assess its real necessity. After meetings, assess again in order to learn for the future.

- ❑ Everyone in attendance was clear on the meeting's purpose.
- ❑ An agenda was provided.
- ❑ The leader controlled the meeting at all times and was fair.
- ❑ The agenda sequence was logical and facilitated understanding.
- ❑ People with varying opinions were able to express them and be heard.
- ❑ Attendees were given the opportunity to add to the agenda.
- ❑ Meeting started and ended on time.
- ❑ Attendees had needed materials prior to the meeting.
- ❑ Time was not wasted by people drifting off the topics, "hogging" the floor, etc.
- ❑ Participants listened to one another.
- ❑ Decisions were made with the input of everyone.
- ❑ The leader summarized decisions and discussions at the end of the meeting.
- ❑ The leader summarized the events and information leading up to the decisions/discussion to refresh participants on the background of the matter under consideration.
- ❑ People trusted one another; they spoke openly without fear of reprisal or attack.
- ❑. Minutes from the last meeting were available.
- ❑ The process used to make decisions or draw conclusions was fair and organized.
- ❑ Follow-up assignments were clearly laid out and coordinated with those involved.
- ❑ Decisions on future meetings or communication exchanges were clearly laid out.

Meeting Evaluation Form for Attendees

To insure that our meetings are a good use of our valuable time, please fill out this assessment so that we can plan more effective meetings in the future. Circle the number you feel best describes our latest meeting:

	Poor				*Good*					*Excellent*
Task Accomplishment	1	2	3	4	5	6	7	8	9	10
Use of Time	1	2	3	4	5	6	7	8	9	10
Use of People's Ideas	1	2	3	4	5	6	7	8	9	10
Conflict Resolution	1	2	3	4	5	6	7	8	9	10
Clear Goal	1	2	3	4	5	6	7	8	9	10
A Sense of Teamwork	1	2	3	4	5	6	7	8	9	10
Effective Listening	1	2	3	4	5	6	7	8	9	10
Keeping on Target	1	2	3	4	5	6	7	8	9	10
HavingNeeded Information	1	2	3	4	5	6	7	8	9	10
Good Decision Making	1	2	3	4	5	6	7	8	9	10
Clear Follow-up Assignments	1	2	3	4	5	6	7	8	9	10
Worth the Time it Took	1	2	3	4	5	6	7	8	9	10

What could be done to make future meetings even more productive?

Self Evaluation Instrument for Volunteer Board/Committee

	Yes	No	Uncertain
1. Do members have a clear sense of the mission of the organization?			
2. Is the mission of the organization clearly focused on solving a clear and current need of the community?			
3. Does the board or committee develop an annual plan of activities?			
4. Is information on current community needs collected before developing the plan?			
5. Does the plan focus on the mission and the goals of the organization?			
6. Does the plan clearly identify goals, objectives, tasks, who will do what, and target dates for review and completion?			
7. Are the work loads in the plan allocated in a realistic and agreed-upon basis?			
8. Are the previous year's objectives and accomplishments reviewed before developing the current year's plan?			
9. Does the plan clearly identify the roles of group members in implementing the plan?			
10. Does the plan allow for a range of activities to be undertaken by volunteers?			
11. Does a mechanism exist for reviewing the activities of board and committee members to ensure that work is being accomplished?			
12. Does the group have a sufficient range of expertise and interests to make it effective?			
13. Do members understand the need to allocate sufficient personal time to accomplish needed work?			
14. Are potential new volunteers to the group informed about their responsibilities between beginning service?			
15. Does the group have a working mechanism for orienting new members about their duties and responsibilities?			
16. Is the group of sufficient size to function effectively?			
17. Do a majority of members attend all meetings?			
18. Does the group meet on a regular basis throughout the year?			

Assessment Tools

	Yes	No	Uncertain

19. Are agendas distributed in advance of meetings?

20. Do members participate in a productive fashion at meetings?

21. Are effective committees and sub-committees established to implement the work of the group?

22. Does the group receive adequate support from the organization to meet its responsibilities?

23. Are meetings commonly spent on the discussion of significant issues on which decisions are to be made?

24. Does the group have an effective method for recruiting new members?

25. Is recruitment of new members directly tied to the organization's needs and plan of activities?

26. Do members possess a high degree of trust and respect for one another?

27. Does the organization have a clearly understood budget which is distributed to all board members and committee members?

28. Does the organization have a clear system for maintaining financial accountability?

29. Do members receive regular financial, policy, and program information of a clear and current nature?

30. Is there a clear understanding of the different roles and responsibilities between the group and other staff and volunteers?

31. Do effective channels of communication exist between the group and other volunteers?

32. Do effective channels of communication exist between the group and staff?

33. Do members seek input from local volunteers, clients, funders, and other concerned groups?

34. Does the leader of the group attempt to involve all members in discussions during meetings?

35. Has there been a high level of turnover among members during recent years?

36. Are most members made to feel that they play a valued role?

37. Do members represent a diverse range of sectors and interests in the community?

38. Do members ever attend and participate in local activities and programs?

Measuring Up:

	Yes	No	Uncertain

39. Do members receive enough information about on-going activities to make intelligent decisions at meetings?

40. Do members and paid staff function effectively as a team?

41. Do members receive adequate staff support for their own work?

42. Does the group operate with a "crisis mentality?"

43. Do some members tend to dominate discussion or decision-making?

44. Do members generally understand the full extent of their own personal commitments and responsibilities?

45. Do some members end up bearing responsibility for a majority of the annual workload?

46. Are meetings dull and boring?

47. Is information about the successes of the organization regularly discussed and shared at meetings?

48. Are problems and barriers to productive involvement of the group openly raised and discussed at meetings?

49. Does the leader of the group exercise authority in a fair and impartial fashion?

50. Are unpleasant tasks rotated among members?

51. Do members express opinions freely and openly during meetings?

52. Are members kept adequately informed between meetings?

53. Do members feel like they are part of a successful team?

54. Does the group leader do a good job of recognizing the contributions of members?

55. Do members accept responsibility for the ultimate success of the organization's mission in their community?

Event Assessment Form for a Committee

Event: *Event date:*

Number of times held: *Dates (years):*

Event Leadership: *In attendance at evaluation meeting:*

1.   What was the overall goal of the event?

2.   List objectives of event and results of each:

     #1:

     #2:

     #3:

     #4:

     #5:

3.   What were strongest/best features of the event?

4.   Where do we see opportunities for improvement?

5.   Do we recommend this event to be held again?

     When?

     With what modifications?

     Suggested leadership:

6.   What benefits came to our organization because of this event?

Project Assessment Form

It is critical that projects are evaluated for impact and efficiency. Such information assists in the decisions about continuing, repeating or dropping efforts and helps in continually improving efforts.

Project: *Begun:*   *Completed:*

Project Leaders: *Key People in Implementation:*

Project Goal:

Objectives:

    1.

    2.

    3.

    4.

    5.

Budget:

Analysis:

1.   Was the project begun and completed on time? If not, explain:

2.   Was budget met? If not, explain:

3.   Was the goal met? If not, explain why. What was learned for future goal attainment?

4.   Describe how the objectives listed above were addressed, including outcomes:

5.   What additional work was needed that was not anticipated?

6.   What took you by surprise as you worked on this project?

7.   What could have predicted these surprises? How can we plan to avoid such surprises in the future?

8.   Often unexpected benefits come out of a project; what were they (if any) with this effort?

9.   What was learned about staffing for this project that can help us plan for personnel in the future?

10. How were results evaluated? What further evaluation needs to be added for the future?

11. How was volunteer or staff performance evaluated? How might we improve on this in the future?

12. What problems arose? How were they handled?

13. How can we improve our problem solving responses in the future?

14. Did any conflicts arise between workers or departments? How were they handled? What were the real issues at stake?

15. How might we structure work in the future to minimize or eliminate such conflicts in the future?

16. Was any technology used in this project? Did it help the success? What might be used in the future?

17. Would you recommend that this project be repeated in the future? Why?

18. Who most benefited from the completion of this effort?

19. What would you do differently if this project is repeated?

20. What would you do the same because it proved essential to success?

21. General comments regarding this project which might be useful for future efforts:

Assessing Hidden Problems in Membership Groups

Signpost	What This Might Indicate
✓ A small group of officers who have been in their positions for many years.	Frozen levels of participation. The small group has unknowingly made it difficult or impossible for others to become actively involved. They will have to be convinced to give up their positions so that others might become involved.
✓ Low attendance at programs or activities.	Could be several problems: inadequate communication with membership about the importance of the activity, poorly run activities that deter people from attending, domination by small group that makes it irrelevant for members to participate. People prefer to volunteer for things they can feel a part of and things that they can have fun with.
✓ Low attendance at meetings	You can't involve them if you can't find them – get the officers to personally invite members to attend, turn the meeting into a real discussion instead of a required event, allow people to have fun and work at the same time.
✓ Same people in charge of everything or of the same things every year.	Frozen levels of participation. Try to convince these leaders to take on assistants and delegate some work and authority. Talk about grooming others to help out in the future.
✓ Group conducts the same activities year after year.	No input from the general membership; domination by a few people who are tired and don't want to try anything new. Get the officers to conduct a needs assessment amongst the membership, or to have a futures planning session at a meeting to generate new ideas. If this is not done it will be harder and harder to involve the membership because they will increasingly see the group as outdated and irrelevant.
✓ Very little discussion at meetings	Domination by a few people. Low interest by general membership. Little attempt to actively involve group. A meeting that is too quiet is usually so because people aren't very interested.
✓ No welcome of new members at meetings.	Officers aren't thinking about new members. New members are thinking about not coming back to another meeting.
✓ Complaints that other officers 'won't do what they're supposed to'.	Usually this is caused by one of two things. The most likely cause is the 'mis-matched' volunteer, a person in a job that they don't want or know how to do. Or it could be caused by a too domineering leader who tries to order, not involve others.
✓ A disorganized group, with no planning calendar, no timelines for activities, little knowledge of guidelines.	This often indicates that the person in charge has taken the job with little inclination to learn how to do it. This is a perfect opportunity for someone to look good, by stepping in and explaining the system to the volunteer and helping them to get organized.

Assessing Potential Success for Fund Raising Efforts

In order to lay the groundwork for the greatest possible success of a fund raiser, a thorough assessment must be done to insure maximum return.

Fund raiser you are considering:

When to be held?

Leadership planned:

Monetary goal:

Event budget:

Subsidiary goals:

1. Have any other such efforts been held in the past?

    * When?
    * Sponsored by:
    * Dollars raised by event:
    * Public perception?

2. What kind of energy would it take to put on such an effort?

    * What leadership from your organization would direct this effort?
    * What other responsibilities do the people listed above also have?
    * Is it realistic to think they can add this effort to their job demands?

3. Given the timing you propose:

    * What other events or efforts would compete for support at the same time internally?
    * What other events or efforts would compete for support at the same time externally?
    * What other calendars must be checked before scheduling? (school, church, holiday, etc.)
    * What alternate dates should be considered if a problem arises?
    * Is there enough time to do all the planning/arranging necessary between now and then?

4. What audience or market segment is targeted as participants?

    * What other fund raisers are also competing for this audience's resources?
    * Do you need lead donors from this audience to publicly commit to the effort?

        ✓ What efforts have been made to sign these key people on?
        ✓ How will you approach them? What will you offer in incentives?
        ✓ What do you expect from them in addition to a lead donation?
        ✓ Who do you think they will influence as future donors?
        ✓ What do you know about them that makes them a likely donor?
        ✓ Who is the best person to approach them? Who is on their level of power?

    * What do you estimate this audience can donate? How do you know this?
    * Are you going to ask for goods-in-kind or manpower commitments?
    * What research has been done about this target audience?

Assessment Tools   **59**

5. How did you select this particular effort?

  - Why do you think it will have public appeal? (Especially target audience.)
  - Do you have information from others who have tried this that can be replicated here?
  - Do you know if you will have public acceptance of this type of effort? How?

6. What marketing or promotion is planned for this effort?

  - Have you sketched out your marketing plan for the effort?
  - What is its timeline? Is this reasonable?
  - Have you researched for the right promotion, price, placement?
  - What ancillary products can be attached to the effort to draw in more revenue?
  - How will you involve the media in promotion? What advertising? Where?

7. What were the budget and revenue projections based on?

  - Are both realistic?
  - Did the people who will run the event participate in the budget discussions?
  - What is the break-even point? How did you arrive at this?
  - If this effort does not make the revenue projected, how will this impact the organization?

8. What are other benefits that the organization can realize in addition to dollars?

  - Gaining a fresh list of supporters to contact later.
  - Good public recognition?
  - Possible recruitment of volunteers?
  - Other:

9. Who is the person ultimately responsible for the success of the event?

  - How involved can they be in directing and managing the effort?
  - Does this leader have the loyalty and support of subordinates who will do the detail work?
  - Does this leader have a management style that will allow subordinates to make decisions?
  - Is it realistic to think this leader can take on this effort in addition to what they already do?
  - Does this person have the authority needed to carry out this effort?

10. Are systems in place that will facilitate (not frustrate) this effort's success?

  - Is decision-making in the hands of a few who would not be directly involved in this effort?
  - Are the systems in the organization simple and direct?
  - Is there a high level of trust among organization staff and volunteers already?
  - What liability and risk issues need to be addressed?
  - What other internal calendars, plans, etc. need to be cleared before starting this effort?
  - Is anyone else in the organization also targeting your audience for support? Who? How? When?

Checklist for a Proposal

✓ **Cover Letter**
- ❑ Briefly describe proposal: purpose, amount, impact
- ❑ Make reference to contact with the grantor in process of development
- ❑ Provide thanks and recognition of previous grants and assistance

✓ **Summary of Proposal**

✓ **Background**
- ❑ Brief description of your organization
- ❑ Your experience with the problem you plan to address
- ❑ How the proposed project fits with your mission
- ❑ Why you are qualified to administer the project

✓ **Problem Statement**
- ❑ Purpose of the request
- ❑ Statement of the urgency of the need
- ❑ Description of the target population
- ❑ Description of other attempts to solve the problem
- ❑ Description of the proposed project
- ❑ How the project fits with the interests of the grantor
- ❑ Benefits the project will produce
- ❑ Relationship to other programs your organization conducts
- ❑ Any collaborative efforts involved with the project

✓ **Project Goals and Objectives**
- ❑ Major project goals
- ❑ Clear, measurable objectives for each goal
- ❑ How objectives will be achieved

✓ **Project Methodology**
- ❑ How the project will be managed and conducted
- ❑ Who will manage the project and their qualifications
- ❑ Expected follow-up for the project

✓ **Project Evaluation**
- ❑ How the project results will be evaluated
- ❑ Frequency and type of reporting to the grantor

✓ **Future Funding Plans**

✓ **Budget**
- ❑ Use format prescribed by the grantor
- ❑ Provide total project budget, with all sources of funds
- ❑ Cite amount requested from this granting source

✓ **Supporting Materials**
- ❑ Proof of tax-exempt status
- ❑ List of board members
- ❑ Support letters

Assessment Tools

Assessing Responsibilities:
An Audit of What You Do

A growing trend in salary and benefit negotiation is the relating of compensation to the responsibilities individual workers and/or departments have within an organization. Identifying the responsibilities you, your key people (volunteer & staff) and your department have is a good exercise no matter what the motivation, because it clarifies all that falls under your jurisdiction.

Such information can be helpful when negotiating with others for support, recruiting volunteers or paid staff, public relations, planning, recognition, accountability, or your own career development. As responsibilities change, you will need to update your audit.

- **Major Responsibilities:**

  I.   Self:

    1.
    2.
    3.
    4.
    5.

  II. Key People You Manage:

    1.
    2.
    3.

  III. Department:

    1.
    2.
    3.

- **Primary Goals:**

    1.
    2.
    3.

- **Budget you oversee:**

- **Other demands:**

    1.
    2.
    3.
    4.

Assessing the Balance in Your Life

As important as it is to assess the various parts of a volunteer program effort, it is just as important to assess the wellness of those who work in the program. Because balancing ones life is critical to wellness, and because the wellness of workers determines the organizational climate within the program, we offer here a simple way to assess balance.

1. List the Most Important People in your life (several can share a #):

#1

#2

#3

#4

#5

2. List your Top Priorities:

#1

#2

#3

#4

#5

3. List your major Stressors: (People or things)

#1`

#2

#3

#4

#5

4. List your major Joys: (People or things)

#1

#2

#3

#4

#5

5. What do you celebrate?

6. What is fun for you to do?

7. Are there things in your past you fret about? (The "should'a, would'a, could'a monsters!)

Now Assess Your Allocation of Your Time:

The climate of an organization is most impacted by the wellness of the people who work within that organization. A major factor in personal wellness is determined by where people spend their time. This assessment tool helps you track where you spend your time...both personally and in working.

In a typical week, I spend "X" (how much?) time with "XX" (name people/things)

- Friends I enjoy:

- Family I enjoy/Love:

- Those who bring me Joy:

- Things I fret about (be specific):

It is also critical that people have time to themselves, to tend to their own special needs. List here the amount of time in a typical week you spend on yourself and what you do in that time:

- In Free-time, just for myself:

- Time for top priorities, joys, celebrations, and fun:

The section above zeroed in on your "Being;" this section tracks the things you "do." In a typical week, how much time would you estimate you are:

Sleeping/eating (10 hrs./day=usual)	*Working*
Traveling	*Volunteering*
Worshipping	*Engaging in hobbies*
Doing chores at home	*Learning*
Socializing	*Being with family*

There can be no universal scoring attached to the above. Only you can determine if your life is properly in balance and if not, how it can regain balance. Some hints for wellness, however:

#1: If your priorities and time allotments don't match, realign them to avoid the frustration at never having time to "get" to your priorities.
#2: Consciously surround yourself with the joys, celebrations and fun you identified.
#3: Let go of things over which you have no control; shake off the hold they have on you.
#4: Does something look out of balance? Are you neglecting an important aspect of your life? How can you spend your time more productively? What steps would help balance your life?

Job Stress Assessment

Effectiveness in programs is dependent in large measure on the wellness of the people involved. Although some stress is necessary for people to feel involved and energized, too much stress drains worker's energies, cuts into creativity and causes good people...especially volunteers...to leave.

The following is a simple assessment tool that indicates levels of stress. Score each statement as:
4 = Almost always   3 = Frequently   2 = Sometimes   1 = Never.

I. Work Environment
1. I have no workspace I can call my own.
2. My work is dangerous or hazardous.
3. I feel great pressure.
4. I am near dangerous substances at work.
5. My workplace is bleak, uncomfortable or depressing.

Total for section:

II. Organizational Environment
1. Office/organizational politics interfere with my work.
2. I can't get the information I need for my work.
3. What is expected is not clear; goals are hazy.
4. There is a negative, backbiting atmosphere.
5. I don't have the resources I need to do my job.
6. I am not part of the decision making process that determines what I am to do.
7. Things are always changing; processes, rules, expectations are different from week to week.
8. I do not see any way to advance.

Total for section:

III. Job Role
1. It is not clear what is expected of me.
2. Too many things are expected of me.
3. I am asked to do things that conflict.
4. I feel overloaded at work.
5. My job expectations are constantly changing.

Total for section:

IV. Self and Role Compatibility
1. I don't like what I do.
2. My job is boring and meaningless.
3. I have the wrong job for me.
4. My job doesn't utilize my skills and abilities.
5. I have ethical problems with what I do.
6. What I wanted/expected from my job has not turned out to be there.
7. I am not able to advance as much as I would like.
8. I have been passed over for promotion.

Total for section:

Score

V. Interpersonal Environment

1. I have too much responsibility for others.
2. Relationships between co-workers, volunteer or staff, are poor and full of conflict.
3. Other people at work create conflict for me.
4. I get no feedback on my work; I'm not sure if others are pleased with me.
5. Too many people tell me what to do.
6. I am pressured by demands of clients/volunteers/supervisors/paid staff.
7. I have too much (or too little) contact with people.
8. I do not like the people I work with.

Total for section:

Analysis

Totals of more than 15 on Sections I & II indicate high stress.

Totals of more than 20 on Sections III, IV & V indicate high stress.

If high stress at work is coupled with high stress in workers personal, financial, legal or relational life, burnout and stress-related problems (health, decision-making, productivity, conflict, etc.) will almost certainly arise

Stress Tolerance Profile

	Never	Rarely	Sometimes	Usually	Always
1. I feel anxiety when a task, project, or mission is not specifically and clearly defined.	1	2	3	4	5
2. If I receive criticism or negative feedback on my work or performance, it leaves me depressed.	1	2	3	4	5
3. Major business decisions make me tense and nervous.	1	2	3	4	5
4. I am very hard-working and aggressive.	1	2	3	4	5
5. A change in routine upsets me.	1	2	3	4	5
6. If one of my subordinates contradicts me, I get uptight and angry.	1	2	3	4	5
7. Pressures and deadlines make me uncomfortable.	1	2	3	4	5
8. When an important future event is scheduled, I begin to 'sweat it out' immediately.	1	2	3	4	5
9. I am punctual and arrive on time for appointments and dates.	1	2	3	4	5
10. Praise from my boss and peers is important to me.	1	2	3	4	5
11. New situations – like a new boss, major policy change, etc. – are stressful.	1	2	3	4	5
12. I'm competitive and determined to be #1 in my department.	1	2	3	4	5
13. When having a problem with a peer or subordinate, I withdraw from the situation or postpone a confrontation.	1	2	3	4	5
14. I am reluctant to reveal anything about my personal life and problems with business associates.	1	2	3	4	5
15. If a method or technique works for me, I'm not apt to alter or change.	1	2	3	4	5
16. I prefer to work alone and not be responsible for or depend on others.	1	2	3	4	5
17. I do work at home in the evenings and on weekends.	1	2	3	4	5
18. During vacations or relaxation, I feel guilty.	1	2	3	4	5
19. Work delays or interruptions annoy me.	1	2	3	4	5
20. When I leave the office at night, my desk is clean and organized.	1	2	3	4	5
Points:	+	+	+	+	=
Total:					

Burnout Quiz

	Does not describe me at all	Describes me somewhat		Describes me very much
1. My standards of performance seem higher than most other people that I work with.	1	2	3	4	5
2. I consider myself to be extremely dedicated and committed to the mission of my work.	1	2	3	4	5
3. I seem to want more intense interactions in my life than most other people I know.	1	2	3	4	5
4. Others tend to see me as highly competent.	1	2	3	4	5
5. I tend to be more of an emotional person than an intellectual, rational person.	1	2	3	4	5
6. I am generally admired by my peers.	1	2	3	4	5
7. I consider myself to be a high energy person.	1	2	3	4	5
8. I have difficulty telling others about my imperfections.	1	2	3	4	5
9. I tend to be more self-critical than self-accepting.	1	2	3	4	5
10. I believe that if I simply try hard enough, I will reach my goals.	1	2	3	4	5
11. I would describe myself more as an extremist than a moderate person in that when I do something, I do it 100 percent.	1	2	3	4	5
12. Once I reach a goal, I rapidly lose the thrill of having achieved it and quickly set my sights on another goal.	1	2	3	4	5
13. I think of myself as persuasive.	1	2	3	4	5
14. Though others may not, I think of myself as an impatient person.	1	2	3	4	5
15. I have trouble delegating tasks that I enjoy but know that others could carry out just as well or almost as well as I do.	1	2	3	4	5

Scoring Key:

15-35	Low potential to burnout
36-55	Moderate potential to burnout
56-75	High potential to burnout